Adobe Illustrator CC Keyboard Shortcuts

By

U. C-Abel Books.

All Rights Reserved

Table of Contents

Acknowledgement. vi

Dedication..vii

How We Began. viii

What to Know Before You Begin. ix

Some Short Forms You Will Find in This Book and Their Full Meaning. xi

1 Fundamental Knowledge of Keyboard Shortcuts. 1

Definition of Computer Keyboard. 1

Ways To Improve In Your Typing Skill. 6

Mouse:...9

Definition Of Keyboard Shortcuts. 11

Why You Should Use Shortcuts. 11

Ways To Become A Lover Of Shortcuts. 12

How To Learn New Shortcut Keys. 13

Your Reward For Knowing Shortcut Keys. 13

Why We Emphasize On The Use of Shortcuts. 14

2 15 (Fifteen) Special Keyboard Shortcuts. 15

3 Tips, Tricks, Techniques, and Keyboard Shortcuts for use in Illustrator. 20

Tools Panel Overview. 20

View hidden tools. 22

View tool options 22

Move the Tools panel 22

View the Tools panel in double-stack or single-column..................... 22

Hide the Tools panel 22

Tear off hidden tools into a separate panel 22

Close a separate tool panel 22

Change Tool Pointers 24

Default Keyboard Shortcuts in Adobe Illustrator........................25

Keys for Selecting Tools.. 25

Keys for Viewing Artwork. 27

Keys for Drawing.. 31

Keys for Drawing in Perspective...................................... 37

Keys for Selecting. 38

Keys for Moving Selections.. 40

Keys for Editing Shapes... 41

Keys for Painting Objects. 43

Keys for working with Live Paint Groups. 45

Keys for Transforming Objects. 47

Keys for Creating Variable Width Points. 48

Keys for Working with Type... 48

Keys for Using Panels.. 51

Keys for the Actions Panel... 52

Keys for the Brushes Panel.. 53

Keys for the Character and Paragraph Panels. 54

Keys for the Color Panel. 55

Keys for the Gradient Panel. 56

Keys for the Layers Panel.. 57

Keys for the Swatches Panel.. 59

Keys for the Transform Panel... 59

Keys for the Transparency Panel. 60

Function Keys.. 61

Customer's Page. 64

Download Our EBooks Today For Free. 65

Other Books By This Publisher.. 67

Acknowledgement.

All thanks to God Almighty for enabling us to bring this work to this point. He is a wonder indeed.

We want to specially appreciate the great company, Adobe Systems Inc. for their hard work and style of reasoning in providing the public with helpful programs and resources, and for helping us with some of the tips and keyboard shortcuts included in this book.

Dedication

The dedication of this title goes to users of
Adobe Illustrator CC.

How We Began.

We enjoy using shortcuts because they set us on a high plane that astonishes people around us when we work with them. As wonderful shortcuts users, the worst eyesore we witness in computer operation is to see somebody sluggishly struggling to execute a task through mouse usage when in actual sense shortcuts will help to save that person time. Most people have asked us to help them with a list of keyboard shortcuts that can make them work as smartly as we do and that drove us into research to broaden our knowledge and truly help them as they demanded, that is the reason for the existence of this book. It is a great tool for lovers of shortcuts, and those who want to join the group.

Most times the things we love don't come by easily. It is our love for keyboard shortcuts that made us to bear long sleepless nights like owls just to make sure we get the best out of it, and it is the best we got that we are sharing with you in this book. You cannot be the same at computing after reading this book. The time you entrusted to our care is an expensive possession and we promise not to mess it up.

Thank you.

What to Know Before You Begin.

General Notes.

1. Most of the keyboard shortcuts you will see in this book refer to the U.S. keyboard layout. Keys for other layouts might not correspond exactly to the keys on a U.S. keyboard. Keyboard shortcuts for laptop computers might also differ.

2. It is important to note that when using shortcuts to perform any command, you should make sure the target area is active, if not, you may get a wrong result. Example, if you want to highlight all texts you must make sure the text field is active and if an object, make sure the object area is active. The active area is always known by the location where the cursor of your computer blinks.

3. On a Mac keyboard, the Command key is denoted with the ⌘symbol.

4. If a function key doesn't work on your Mac as you expect it to, press the Fn key in addition to the function key. If you don't want to press the Fn key every time, you can change your Apple system preferences.

5. The plus (+) sign that comes in the middle of keyboard shortcuts simply means the keys are

meant to be combined or held down together not to be added as one of the shortcut keys. In a case where plus sign is needed; it will be duplicated (++).

6. Many keyboards assign special functions to function keys, by default. To use the function key for other purposes, you have to press Fn+the function key.

7. For keyboard shortcuts in which you press one key immediately followed by another key, the keys are separated by a comma (,).

8. For chapters that have more than one topic, search for "A fresh topic" to see the beginning of a topic, and "End of Topic" to see the end of a topic.

9. It is also important to note that the keyboard shortcuts, tips, and techniques listed in this book are for use in Adobe Illustrator CC.

10. To get more information on this title visit <u>ucabelbooks.wordpress.com</u> and search the site using keywords related to it.

11. Our chief website is under construction.

Some Short Forms You Will Find in This Book and Their Full Meaning.

Here are short forms used in this Adobe Illustrator CC Keyboard Shortcuts book and their full meaning.

1.	Win	-	Windows logo key
2.	Tab	-	Tabulate Key
3.	Shft	-	Shift Key
4.	Prt sc	-	Print Screen
5.	Num Lock	-	Number Lock Key
6.	F	-	Function Key
7.	Esc	-	Escape Key
8.	Ctrl	-	Control Key
9.	Caps Lock	-	Caps Lock Key
10.	Alt	-	Alternate Key

CHAPTER 1.

Fundamental Knowledge of Keyboard Shortcuts.

Without the existence of the keyboard, there wouldn't have been anything like keyboard shortcuts so in this chapter we will learn a little about the computer keyboard before moving to keyboard shortcuts.

1. Definition of Computer Keyboard.

This is an input device that is used to send data to computer memory.

Sketch of a Keyboard

1.1 Types of Keyboard.

   i. Standard (Basic) Keyboard.
  ii. Enhanced (Extended) Keyboard.

   i. **Standard Keyboard:** This is a keyboard designed during the 1800s for mechanical typewriters with just 10 function keys (F keys) placed at the left side of it.

  ii. **Enhanced Keyboard:** This is the current 101 to 102-key keyboard that is included in almost all the personal computers (PCs) of nowadays, which has 12 function keys, usually at the top side of it.

1.2 Segments of the keyboard

- Numeric keys.
- Alphabetic keys.
- Punctuation keys.
- Windows Logo key.
- Function keys.
- Special keys.

Numeric Keys: Numeric keys are keys with numbers from **0 - 9**.

Alphabetic Keys: These are keys that have alphabets on them, ranging from **A** to **Z**.

Punctuation Keys: These are keys of the keyboard used for punctuation, examples include comma, full stop, colon, question marks, hyphen, etc.

Windows Logo Key: A key on Microsoft Computer keyboard with its logo displayed on it. Search for this ⊞ on your keyboard.

Apple Key: This also known as Command key is a modifier key that you can find on an Apple keyboard. It usually has the image of an apple or command logo on it. Search for this on your Apple keyboard ⌘

Function Keys: These are keys that have **F** on them which are usually combined with other keys. They are F1 - F12, and are also in the class called *Special Keys*.

Special Keys: These are keys that perform special functions. They include: Tab, Ctrl, Caps lock, Insert, Prt sc, alt gr, Shift, Home, Num lock, Esc, and many others. Special keys differ according to the type of computer involved. In some keyboard layout, especially laptops, the keys that turn the speaker on/off, the one that increases/decreases volume, the key that turns the computer Wifi on/off are also special keys.

Other Special Keys Worthy of Note.

Enter Key: This is located at the right-hand corner of most keyboards. It is used to send messages to the computer to execute commands, in most cases it is used to mean "Ok" or "Go".

Escape Key (ESC): This is the first key on the upper left of most keyboards. It is used to cancel routines, close menus and select options such as **Save** according to circumstances.

Control Key (CTRL): It is located on the bottom row of the left and right hand side of the keyboard. They also work with the function keys to execute commands using Keyboard shortcuts (key combinations).

Alternate Key (ALT): It is located on the bottom row also of some keyboard, very close to the CTRL key on both side of the keyboard. It enables many editing functions to be accomplished by using some keystroke combinations on the keyboard.

Shift Key: This adds to the roles of function keys. In addition, it enables the use of alternative function of a particular button (key), especially, those with more than one function on a key. E.g. use of capital letters, symbols, and numbers.

1.3. Selecting/Highlighting With Keyboard.

This is a highlighting method or style where data is selected using the computer keyboard instead of a computer mouse.

To do this:

- Move your cursor to the text or object you want to highlight, make sure that area is active,
- Hold down the shift key with one finger,
- Then use another finger to move the arrow key that points to the direction you want to highlight.

1.4 The Operating Modes Of The Keyboard.

Just like the computer mouse, keyboard has two operating modes. The two modes are Text Entering Mode and Command Mode.

a.   **Text Entering Mode:** this mode gives the operator/user the opportunity to type text.
b.   **Command Mode:** this is used to command the operating system/software/application to execute commands in certain ways.

2. Ways To Improve In Your Typing Skill.

1. Put Your Eyes Off The Keyboard.

This is the aspect of keyboard usage that many don't find funny because they always ask. "How can I put my eyes off the keyboard when I am running away from the occurrence of errors on my file?" My aim is to be fast, is this not going to slow me down?

Of course, there will be errors and at the same time your speed will slow down but the motive behind the introduction to this method is to make you faster than you are. Looking at your keyboard while you type can make you get a sore neck, it is better you learn to touch type because the more you type with your eyes fixed on the screen instead of the keyboard, the faster you become.

An alternative to keeping your eyes off your keyboard is to use the "*Das Keyboard Ultimate*".

2. Errors Challenge You

It is better to fail than to not try at all. Not trying at all is an attribute of the weak and lazybones. When you make mistakes, try again because errors are opportunities for improvement.

3. Good Posture (Position Yourself Well).

Do not adopt an awkward position while typing. You should get everything on your desk organized or arranged before sitting to type. Your posture while typing contributes to your speed and productivity.

4. Practice

Here is the conclusion of everything said above. You have to practice your shortcuts constantly. The practice alone is a way of improvement. "Practice brings improvement". Practice always.

2.1 Software That Will Help You Improve Your Typing Skill.

There are several Software programs for typing that both kids and adults can use for their typing skill. Here is a list of software that can help you improve in your typing: Mavis Beacon, Typing Instructor, Mucky Typing Adventure, Rapid Tying Tutor, Letter Chase Tying Tutor, Alice Touch Typing Tutor and many more. Personally, I love Mavis Beacon.

To learn typing using MAVIS BEACON, install Mavis Beacon software to your computer, start with keyboard lesson, then move to games. Games like **Penguin Crossing, Creature Lab**, or **Space Junk** will help you become a professional in typing. Typing and keyboard shortcuts work hand-in-hand.

Sketch of a computer mouse

Right Mouse button

Scroll button

Left Mouse button

3. Mouse:

This is an oval-shaped portable input device with three buttons for scrolling, left clicking, and right clicking that enables work to be done effectively on a computer. The plural form of mouse is mice.

3.1 Types of Computer Mouse

- Mechanical Mouse.
- Optical Mechanical Mouse (Optomechanical).
- Laser Mouse.

9

- Optical Mouse.
- BlueTrack Mouse.

3.2 Forms of Clicking:

Left Clicking: This is the process of clicking the left side button of the mouse. It can also be called *clicking* without the addition of *left*.

Right Clicking: It is the process of clicking the right side button of a computer mouse.

Double Clicking: It is the process of clicking the left side button two times (twice) and immediately.

Triple Clicking: It is the process of clicking the left side button three times (thrice) and immediately.

Double clicking is used to select a word while triple clicking is used to select a sentence or paragraph.

Scroll Button: It is the little key attached to the mouse that looks like a tiny wheel. It takes you up and down a page when moved.

3.3 Mouse Pad: This is a small soft mat that is placed under the mouse to make it have a free movement.

3.4 Laptop Mouse Touchpad

This unlike the mouse we explained above is not external, rather it is inbuilt (comes with the laptop computer). With the presence of a laptop mouse touchpad, an external mouse is not needed to use a laptop, except in a case where it is malfunctioning or the operator prefers to use external one for some reasons.

The laptop mouse touchpad is usually positioned at the end of the keyboard section of a laptop computer. It is rectangular in shape with two buttons positioned below it. The two buttons/keys are used for left and right clicking just like the external mouse. Some laptops come with four mouse keys. Two placed above the mouse for left and right clicking and two other keys placed below it for the same function.

4. Definition Of Keyboard Shortcuts.

Keyboard shortcuts are defined as a series of keys, most times with combination that execute tasks which typically involve the use of mouse or other input devices.

5. Why You Should Use Shortcuts.

1. One may not be able to use a computer mouse easily because of disability or pain.

2. One may not be able to see the mouse pointer as a result of vision impairment, in such case what will the person do? The answer is SHORTCUT.

3. Research has made it known that Extensive mouse usage is related to Repetitive Syndrome Injury (RSI) greatly than the use of keyboard.

4. Keyboard shortcuts speed up computer users, making learning them a worthwhile effort.

5. When performing a job that requires precision, it is wise that you use the keyboard instead of mouse, for instance, if you are dealing with Text Editing, it is better you handle it using keyboard shortcuts than spending more time doing it with your computer mouse alone.

6. Studies calculate that using keyboard shortcuts allows working 10 times faster than working with the mouse. The time you spend looking for the mouse and then getting the cursor to the position you want is lost! Reducing your work duration by 10 times gives you greater results.

5.1 Ways To Become A Lover Of Shortcuts.

1. Always have the urge to learn new shortcut keys associated with the programs you use.
2. Be happy whenever you learn a new shortcut.

3. Try as much as you can to apply the new shortcuts you learnt.
4. Always bear it in mind that learning new shortcuts is worth it.
5. Always remember that the use of keyboard shortcuts keeps people healthy while performing computer activities.

5.2 How To Learn New Shortcut Keys

1. Do a research on them: quick references (a cheat sheet comprehensively compiled like ours) can go a long way to help you improve.
2. Buy applications that show you keyboard shortcuts every time you execute an action with mouse.
3. Disconnect your mouse if you must learn this fast.
4. Read user manuals and help topics (Whether offline or online).

5.3 Your Reward For Knowing Shortcut Keys.

1. You will get faster unimaginably.
2. Your level of efficiency will increase.
3. You will find it easy to use.
4. Opportunities are high that you will become an expert in what you do.
5. You won't have to go for **Office button**, click **New,** click **Blank and Recent**, and click **Create**

just to insert a fresh/blank page. **Ctrl +N** takes care of that in a second.

A Funny Note: Keyboarding and Mousing are in a marital union with Keyboarding being the head, so it will be unfair for anybody to put asunder between them.

5.4 Why We Emphasize On The Use of Shortcuts.

You may never leave your mouse completely unless you are ready to make your brain a box of keyboard shortcuts which will really be frustrating, just imagine yourself learning all shortcuts that go with the programs you use and their various versions. You shouldn't learn keyboard shortcuts that way.

Why we are emphasizing on the use of shortcuts is because mouse usage is becoming unusually common and unhealthy, too. So we just want to make sure both are combined so you can get fast, productive and healthy in your computer activities. All you need to know is just the most important ones associated with the programs you use.

CHAPTER 2.

15 (Fifteen) Special Keyboard Shortcuts.

The fifteen special keyboard shortcuts are fifteen (15) shortcuts every computer user should know.

The following is a list of keyboard shortcuts every computer user should know:

1. **Ctrl + A:** Control A, highlights or selects everything you have in the environment where you are working.

   If you are like **"Wow, the content of this document is large and there is no time to select all of it, besides, it's going to mount pressure on my computer?"** *Using the mouse for this is an outdated method of handling a task like selecting all, Ctrl+A will take care of that in a second.*

2. **Ctrl + C:** Control C copies any highlighted or selected element within the work environment.

> *Saves the time and stress which would have been used to right click and click again just to copy. Use ctrl+c.*

3. **Ctrl + N:** Control N opens a new window or file.

> *Instead of clicking* **File**, **New**, **blank/ template** *and another* **click**, *just press* **Ctrl + N** *and a fresh page or window will appear instantly.*

4. **Ctrl + O:** Control O opens a new program.

> *Use ctrl +O when you want to locate / open a file or program.*

5. **Ctrl + P:** Control P prints the active document.

> *Always use this to locate the printer dialog box, and thereafter print.*

6. **Ctrl + S:** Control S saves a new document or file and changes made by the user.

> *Please stop! Don't use the mouse. Just press Ctrl+S and everything will be saved.*

7. **Ctrl +V:** Control V pastes copied elements into the active area of the program in use.

Using ctrl+V in a case like this Saves the time and stress of right clicking and clicking again just to paste.

8. **Ctrl + W:** Control W is used to close the page you are working on when you want to leave the work environment.

    "There is a way Debby does this without using the mouse. Oh my God, why didn't I learn it then?" Don't worry, I have the answer. Debby presses Ctrl+W to close active windows.

9. **Ctrl + X:** Control X cuts elements (making the elements to disappear from their original place). The difference between cutting and deleting elements is that in Cutting, what was cut doesn't get lost permanently but prepares itself so that it can be pasted on another location defined by the user.

    *Use ctrl+x when you think **"this shouldn't be here and I can't stand the stress of retyping or redesigning it on the rightful place it belongs".***

10. **Ctrl + Y:** Control Y undoes already done actions.

    Ctrl+Z brought back what you didn't need? Press Ctrl+ Y to remove it again.

17

11. **Ctrl + Z:** Control Z redoes actions.

Can't find what you typed now or a picture you inserted, it suddenly disappeared or you mistakenly removed it? Press Ctrl+Z to bring it back.

12. **Alt + F4:** Alternative F4 closes active windows or items.

*You don't need to move the mouse in order to close an active window, just press **Alt + F4**. Also use it when you are done or you don't want somebody who is coming to see what you are doing.*

13. **Ctrl + F6:** Control F6 Navigates between open windows, making it possible for a user to see what is happening in windows that are active.

Are you working in Microsoft Word and want to find out if the other active window where your browser is loading a page is still progressing? Use Ctrl + F6.

14. **F1:** This displays the help window.

*Is your computer malfunctioning? Use **F1** to find help when you don't know what next to do.*

15. **F12:** This enables user to make changes to an already saved document.

> *F12 is the shortcut to use when you want to change the format in which you saved your existing document, password it, change its name, change the file location or destination, or make other changes to it. It will save you time.*

Note: The Control (Ctrl) key on Windows and Linux operating system is the same thing as Command (Cmmd) key on a Macintosh computer. So if you replace Control with Command key on a Mac computer for the special shortcuts listed above, you will get the same result.

CHAPTER 3.

Tips, Tricks, Techniques, and Keyboard Shortcuts for use in Illustrator CC.

About the program: This is a program used by graphics designers and artists for the creation of vector images, developed by Adobe Systems.

A fresh topic

Tools Panel Overview.

The first time you start the application, the Tools panel appears at the left side of the screen. You can move the Tools panel by dragging its title bar. You can also show or hide the Tools panel by choosing Window > Tools.

You use tools in the Tools panel to create, select, and manipulate objects in Illustrator. Some tools have options that appear when you double-click a tool. These include tools that let you use type, and select, paint, draw, sample, edit, and move images.

You can expand some tools to show hidden tools beneath them. A small triangle at the lower-right corner of the tool icon signals the presence of hidden tools. To see the name of a tool, position the pointer over it.

You can also use the Tools panel to change the drawing mode from Draw Normal to Draw Behind or Draw Inside.

Tools panel overview

View hidden tools.

- Hold down the mouse button on the visible tool.

View tool options

- Double-click a tool in the Tools panel.

Move the Tools panel

- Drag its title bar.

View the Tools panel in double-stack or single-column

- Click the double-arrow on the title bar to toggle between double-stack and single-column view of the Tools panel.

Hide the Tools panel

- Choose Window > Tools.

Tear off hidden tools into a separate panel

- Drag the pointer over the arrow at the end of the hidden tools panel and release the mouse button.

Close a separate tool panel

- Click the close button on the panel's title bar. The tools return to the Tools panel.

Select a tool

- Do one of the following:
  - Click a tool in the Tools panel. If there is a small triangle at a tool's lower-right corner, hold down the mouse button to view the hidden tools, and then click the tool you want to select.
  - Hold down Alt (Windows) or Option (Mac OS), and then click a tool to cycle through and select hidden tools.
  - Press the tool's keyboard shortcut. The keyboard shortcut is displayed in its tool tip. For example, you can select the Move tool by pressing the V key.

    Tip*: To hide tool tips, choose Edit > Preferences > General (Windows) or Illustrator > Preferences > General (Mac OS), and deselect Show Tool Tips.*

- Selecting a hidden tool

  A. Tools panel **B.** Active tool **C.** Tear off panel with hidden tools **D.** Hidden tool triangle **E.** Tool name and shortcut

Change Tool Pointers.

The mouse pointer for most tools matches the tool's icon. Each pointer has a different hotspot, where an effect or action begins. With most tools, you can switch to precise cursors, which appear as cross hairs centered around the hotspot, and provide for greater accuracy when working with detailed artwork.

- Choose Edit > Preferences > General (Windows) or Illustrator > Preferences > General (Mac OS), and select Use Precise Cursors. Alternatively, press Caps Lock on the keyboard.

-by Adobe Systems Inc. experts.

End of Topic.

A fresh topic

Default Keyboard Shortcuts in Adobe Illustrator.

Use the following list of keyboard shortcuts to enhance your productivity in Adobe Illustrator.

Keys for Selecting Tools.

Result	Windows Shortcut	Mac OS Shortcut
Artboard tool	Shift + O	Shift + O
Selection tool	V	V
Direct Selection tool	A	A
Magic Wand tool	Y	Y
Lasso tool	Q	Q
Pen tool	P	P

Blob Brush tool	Shift + B	Shift + B
Add Anchor Point tool	+ (plus)	+ (plus)
Delete Anchor Point tool	- (minus)	- (minus)
Convert Anchor Point tool	Shift + C	Shift + C
Type tool	T	T
Line Segment tool	\ (backslash)	\ (backslash)
Rectangle tool	M	M
Ellipse tool	L	L
Paintbrush tool	B	B
Pencil tool	N	N
Rotate tool	R	R
Reflect tool	O	O
Scale tool	S	S
Warp tool	Shift + R	Shift + R
Width Tool	Shift+W	Shift+W
Free Transform tool	E	E
Shape Builder Tool	Shift+M	Shift+M
Perspective Grid Tool	Shift+P	Shift+P
Perspective Selection Tool	Shift+V	Shift+V
Symbol Sprayer tool	Shift + S	Shift + S
Column Graph tool	J	J
Mesh tool	U	U
Gradient tool	G	G
Eyedropper tool	I	I
Blend tool	W	W

Live Paint Bucket tool	K	K
Live Paint Selection tool	Shift + L	Shift + L
Slice tool	Shift + K	Shift + K
Eraser tool	Shift + E	Shift + E
Scissors tool	C	C
Hand tool	H	H
Zoom tool	Z	Z
Switch to Smooth tool while using Blob Brush tool	Press Alt	Press Option

Keys for Viewing Artwork.

This is not a complete list of keyboard shortcuts. This table lists only those shortcuts that are not displayed in menu commands or tool tips.

Result	Windows Shortcut	Mac OS Shortcut
Toggle between screen modes: Normal Screen Mode, Full Screen	F	F

Mode with Menu Bar, Full Screen Mode		
Fit imageable area in window	Double-click Hand tool	Double-click Hand tool
Magnify 100%	Double-click Zoom tool	Double-click Zoom tool
Switch to Hand tool (when not in text-edit mode)	Spacebar	Spacebar
Switch to Zoom tool in magnify mode	Ctrl + Spacebar	Spacebar + Command
Switch to Zoom tool in reduce mode	Ctrl + Alt + Spacebar	Spacebar + Command + Option
Move Zoom marquee	Spacebar	Spacebar

while dragging with the Zoom tool		
Hide unselected artwork	Control + Alt + Shift + 3	Command + Option + Shift + 3
Convert between horizontal and vertical guide	Alt-drag guide	Option-drag guide
Release guide	Ctrl + Shift-double-click guide	Command + Shift-double-click guide
Show/Hide artboards	Ctrl + Shift + H	Command + Shift + H
Show/Hide artboard rulers	Ctrl + Alt + R	Command + Option + R
View all artboards in window	Ctrl + Alt + 0 (zero)	Command + Option + 0 (zero)
Paste in place on the active artboard	Ctrl+Shift+V	Command+Shift+V

Exit Artboard tool mode	Esc	Esc
Create artboard inside another artboard	Shift-drag	Shift-drag
Select multiple artboards in the Artboards panel	Ctrl+click	Command+click
Navigate to next document	Ctrl + F6	Command+F6
Navigate to previous document	Ctrl + Shift + F6	Command+Shift+F6
Navigate to next document group	Ctrl + Alt + F6	Command+Option+F6
Navigate to previous document group	Ctrl + Alt + Shift + F6	Command+Option+Shift+ F6

Exit Full Screen mode	Esc	Esc
Save multiple artboards to Illustrator CS3 or earlier format	Alt + v	

Keys for Drawing.

This is not a complete list of keyboard shortcuts. This table lists only those shortcuts that are not displayed in menu commands or tool tips.

Result	Windows Shortcut	Mac OS Shortcut
Constrain a shape's proportions or orientation to: • equal height and width for	Shift-drag	Shift-drag

rectangles, rounded rectangles, ellipses, and grids • Increments of 45° for line and arc segments • Original orientation for polygons, stars, and flares		
Move a shape while drawing it	spacebar-drag	spacebar-drag
Draw from the center of a	Alt-drag	Option-drag

shape (except for polygons, stars, and flares)		
Increase or decrease polygon sides, star points, arc angle, spiral winds, or flare rays	Start dragging, then press the Up Arrow or Down Arrow	Start dragging, then press the Up Arrow or Down Arrow
Keep the inner radius of a star constant	Start dragging, then hold down Ctrl	Start dragging, then hold down Command
Keep the sides of a star straight	Alt-drag	Option-drag
Switch between an open and closed arc	Start dragging, then hold down C	Start dragging, then hold down C
Flip an arc, keeping the reference point constant	Start dragging, then hold down F	Start dragging, then hold down SF
Add or subtract winds from a	Start dragging,	Start dragging then Option-drag

spiral while increasing the length of the spiral	then Alt-drag	
Change the decay rate of a spiral	Start dragging then Ctrl-drag	Start dragging then Command-drag
Add or remove horizontal lines from a rectangular grid or concentric lines from a polar grid	Start dragging, then press the Up Arrow or Down Arrow	Start dragging, then press the Up Arrow or Down Arrow
Add or remove vertical lines from a rectangular grid or radial lines from a polar grid	Start dragging, then press the Right Arrow or Left Arrow	Start dragging, then press the Right Arrow or Left Arrow
Decrease the skew value for horizontal dividers in a rectangular grid or radial	Start dragging, then press F	Start dragging, then press F

dividers in a polar grid by 10%		
Increase the skew value for horizontal dividers in a rectangular grid or radial dividers in a polar grid by 10%	Start dragging, then press V	Start dragging, then press V
Decrease the skew value for vertical dividers in a rectangular grid or concentric dividers in a polar grid by 10%	Start dragging, then press X	Start dragging, then press X
Increase the skew value for vertical dividers in a rectangular grid or concentric dividers in a	Start dragging, then press C	Start dragging, then press C

polar grid by 10%		
Create and expand a Live Trace object in one step	Alt-click Live Trace in the Control panel, or hold down Alt and select a tracing preset.	Option-click Live Trace in the Control panel, or hold down Option and select a tracing preset.
Increase size of Blob Brush	] (right square bracket)	] (right square bracket)
Decrease size of Blob Brush	[(left square bracket)	[(left square bracket)
Constrain Blob Brush path horizontally or vertically	Shift	Shift
Switch through drawing modes	Shift+D	Shift+D
Join two or more paths	Select the paths, then press Ctrl+J	Select the paths, then press Command+J
Create corner or smooth join	Select the paths, then press	Select the anchor point, then press Shift+Command+Option+j

	Shift+Ctrl+Alt+j	

Keys for Drawing in Perspective.

This is not a complete list of keyboard shortcuts. This table lists only those shortcuts that are not displayed in menu commands or tool tips.

Results	Windows Shortcut	Mac OS Shortcut
Perspective Grid Tool	Shift+P	Shift+P
Perspective Selection Tool	Shift+V	Shift+V
Perspective Grid	Ctrl+Shift+I	Command+Shift+I
Moving objects perpendicularly	Press the number 5 key, then click and drag the object	Press the number 5 key, then click and drag the object
Switching perspective planes	Use the Perspective Selection tool and then press 1 for left grid, 2 for horizontal	Use the Perspective Selection tool and then press 1 for left grid, 2 for horizontal grid, 3 for right grid, or 4 for no active grid

	grid, 3 for right grid, or 4 for no active grid	
Copying objects in perspective	Ctrl+Alt+drag	Command+Alt+drag
Repeat transforming objects in perspective	Ctrl+D	Command+D
Switching between drawing modes	Shift+D	Shift+D

Keys for Selecting.

This is not a complete list of keyboard shortcuts. This table lists only those shortcuts that are not displayed in menu commands or tool tips.

Result	Windows Shortcut	Mac OS Shortcut
Switch to last-used selection tool (Selection tool, Direct Selection tool, or Group Selection tool)	Ctrl	Command

Switch between Direct Selection tool and Group Selection tool	Alt	Option
Add to a selection with Selection tool, Direct Selection tool, Group Selection tool, Live Paint Selection tool, or Magic Wand tool	Shift-click	Shift-click
Subtract a selection with Selection tool, Direct Selection tool, Group Selection tool, or LIve Paint Selection tool	Shift-click	Shift-click
Subtract from selection with Magic Wand tool	Alt-click	Option-click
Add to selection with Lasso tool	Shift-drag	Shift-drag
Subtract from selection with Lasso tool	Alt-drag	Option-drag
Change pointer to cross hair for Lasso tool	Caps Lock	Caps Lock

Select artwork in active artboard	Ctrl + Alt + A	Command + Option + A
Create crop marks around selected object	Alt + c + o	
Select behind an object	Press Ctrl+click twice	Press Command+click twice
Select behind in isolation mode	Ctrl+click twice	Command+click twice

Keys for Moving Selections.

This is not a complete list of keyboard shortcuts. This table lists only those shortcuts that are not displayed in menu commands or tool tips.

Result	Windows Shortcut	Mac OS Shortcut
Move selection in user-defined increments	Right Arrow, Left Arrow, Up Arrow, or Down Arrow	Right Arrow, Left Arrow, Up Arrow, or Down Arrow
Move selection in 10x user-defined increments	Shift + Right Arrow, Left Arrow, Up Arrow, or Down Arrow	Shift + Right Arrow, Left Arrow, Up Arrow, or Down Arrow

Lock all deselected artwork	Ctrl + Alt + Shift + 2	Command + Option + Shift + 2
Constrain movement to 45° angle (except when using Reflect tool)	Hold down Shift	Hold down Shift

Note:

Set keyboard increments in General Preferences

Keys for Editing Shapes.

This is not a complete list of keyboard shortcuts. This table lists only those shortcuts that are not displayed in menu commands or tool tips.

Result	Windows Shortcut	Mac OS Shortcut
Switch Pen tool to Convert Anchor Point tool	Alt	Option
Switch between Add Anchor Point tool and	Alt	Option

Delete Anchor Point tool		
Switch Scissors tool to Add Anchor Point tool	Alt	Option
Switch Pencil tool to Smooth tool	Alt	Option
Move current anchor point while drawing with Pen tool	Spacebar-drag	Spacebar-drag
Cut a straight line with Knife tool	Alt-drag	Option-drag
Cut at 45° or 90° with Knife tool	Shift + Alt-drag	Shift + Option-drag
Use shape mode buttons in Pathfinder panel to create compound paths	Alt + Shape mode	Option + Shape mode
Erase unwanted closed regions created using	Alt+click the closed region	Option+click the closed region

Shape Builder tool		
Select the Shape Builder tool	Shift+M	Shift+M
Display rectangular marquee to easily merge multiple paths (when using Shape Builder tool)	Shift+click+drag	Shift+click+drag

Keys for Painting Objects.

This is not a complete list of keyboard shortcuts. This table lists only those shortcuts that are not displayed in menu commands or tool tips.

Result	Windows Shortcut	Mac OS Shortcut
Toggle between fill and stroke	X	X
Set fill and stroke to default	D	D
Swap fill and stroke	Shift + X	Shift + X
Select gradient fill mode	>	>

Select color fill mode	<	<
Select no stroke/fill mode	/ (forward slash)	/ (forward slash)
Sample color from an image or intermediate color from gradient	Shift + Eyedropper tool	Shift + Eyedropper tool
Sample style and append appearance of currently selected item	Alt + Shift-click + Eyedropper tool	Option + Shift-click + Eyedropper tool
Add new fill	Ctrl + / (forward slash)	Command + / (forward slash)
Add new stroke	Ctrl + Alt + / (forward slash)	Command + Option + / (forward slash)
Reset gradient to black and white	Ctrl-click gradient button in Tools panel or Gradient panel	Command-click gradient button in Tools panel or Gradient panel
Open Mosaic options for selected raster object	Alt + o + j	
Decrease Bristle brush size	[	[

Increase Bristle brush size	]	]
Set Bristle brush paint opacity value	Number keys 1 - 0. Number key 1 increases the value to 10% Number key 0 increases the value to 100%	Number keys 1 - 0. Number key 1 increases the value to 10% Number key 0 increases the value to 100%

Keys for Working with Live Paint Groups.

This is not a complete list of keyboard shortcuts. This table lists only those shortcuts that are not displayed in menu commands or tool tips.

Result	Windows Shortcut	Mac OS Shortcut
Switch to Eyedropper tool and sample fill and/or stroke	Alt-click + Live Paint Bucket tool	Option-click + Live Paint Bucket tool
Switch to Eyedropper tool and sample color from an image or intermediate color from a gradient	Alt + Shift-click + Live Paint Bucket tool	Option + Shift-click + Live Paint Bucket tool

Select opposite Live Paint Bucket tool options (if Paint Fills and Paint Strokes are currently selected, switch to Paint Fills only)	Shift + Live Paint Bucket tool	Shift + Live Paint Bucket tool
Fill across unstroked edges into adjacent faces	Double-click + Live Paint Bucket tool	Double-click + Live Paint Bucket tool
Fill all faces that have same fill and stroke all edges that have same stroke	Triple-click + Live Paint Bucket tool	Triple-click + Live Paint Bucket tool
Switch to Eyedropper tool and sample fill and/or stroke	Alt-click + Live Paint Selection tool	Option-click + Live Paint Selection tool
Switch to Eyedropper tool and sample color from an image or intermediate color from a gradient	Alt + Shift-click + Live Paint Selection tool	Option + Shift-click + Live Paint Selection tool
Add to/subtract from a selection	Shift-click + Live Paint Selection tool	Shift-click + Live Paint Selection tool
Select all connected faces /edges with same fill/stroke	Double-click + Live Paint Selection tool	Double-click + Live Paint Selection tool

| Select all faces/edges with same fill/stroke | Triple-click + Live Paint Selection tool | Triple-click + Live Paint Selection tool |

Keys for Transforming Objects.

This is not a complete list of keyboard shortcuts. This table lists only those shortcuts that are not displayed in menu commands or tool tips.

Result	Windows Shortcut	Mac OS Shortcut
Set origin point and open dialog box when using Rotate tool, Scale tool, Reflect tool, or Shear tool	Alt-click	Option-click
Duplicate and transform selection when using Selection tool, Scale tool, Reflect tool, or Shear tool	Alt-drag	Option-drag
Transform pattern (independent of object) when using Selection tool, Scale tool, Reflect tool, or Shear tool	Tilde (~)-drag	Tilde (~)-drag

Keys for Creating Variable Width Points.

This is not a complete list of keyboard shortcuts. This table lists only those shortcuts that are not displayed in menu commands or tool tips.

Results	Windows Shortcut	Mac OS Shortcut
Select multiple width points	Shift+click	Shift+click
Create non-uniform widths	Alt+drag	Option+drag
Create a copy of the width point	Alt+drag the width point	Options+drag the width point
Change the position of multiple width points	Shift+drag	Shift+drag
Delete selected width point	Delete	Delete
Deselect a width point	Esc	Esc

Keys for Working with Type.

This is not a complete list of keyboard shortcuts. This table lists only those shortcuts that are not displayed in menu commands or tool tips.

Result	Windows Shortcut	Mac OS Shortcut
Move one character right or left	Right Arrow or Left Arrow	Right Arrow or Left Arrow
Move up or down one line	Up Arrow or Down Arrow	Up Arrow or Down Arrow
Move one word right or left	Ctrl + Right Arrow or Left Arrow	Command + Right Arrow or Left Arrow
Move up or down one paragraph	Ctrl + Up Arrow or Down Arrow	Command + Up Arrow or Down Arrow
Select one word right or left	Shift + Ctrl + Right Arrow or Left Arrow	Shift + Command + Right Arrow or Left Arrow
Select one paragraph before or after	Shift + Ctrl + Up Arrow or Down Arrow	Shift + Command + Up Arrow or Down Arrow
Extend existing selection	Shift-click	Shift-click
Align paragraph left, right, or center	Ctrl + Shift + L, R, or C	Command + Shift + L, R, or C
Justify paragraph	Ctrl + Shift + J	Command + Shift + J
Insert soft return	Shift + Enter	Shift + Return
Highlight kerning	Ctrl + Alt + K	Command + Option + K

Reset horizontal scale to 100%	Ctrl + Shift + X	Command + Shift + X
Increase or decrease type size	Ctrl + Shift + > or <	Command + Shift + > or <
Increase or decrease leading	Alt + Up or Down Arrow (horizontal text) or Right or Left Arrow (vertical text)	Option + Up or Down Arrow (horizontal text) or Right or Left Arrow (vertical text)
Reset tracking/kerning to 0	Ctrl + Alt + Q	Command + Option + Q
Increase or decrease kerning and tracking	Alt + Right or Left Arrow (horizontal text) or Up or Down Arrow (vertical text)	Option + Right or Left Arrow (horizontal text) or Up or Down Arrow (vertical text)
Increase or decrease kerning and tracking by five times	Ctrl + Alt + Right or Left Arrow (horizontal text) or Up or Down Arrow (vertical text)	Command + Option + Right or Left Arrow (horizontal text) or Up or Down Arrow (vertical text)
Increase or decrease baseline shift	Alt + Shift + Up or Down	Option + Shift + Up or Down

	Arrow (horizontal text) or Right or Left Arrow (vertical text)	Arrow (horizontal text) or Right or Left Arrow (vertical text)
Switch between Type and Vertical Type, Area Type and Vertical Area Type, and Path Type and Vertical Path Type tools	Shift	Shift
Switch between Area Type and Path Type, Vertical Area Type and Vertical Path Type tools	Alt	Option

Note:

To change the increment value for type shortcuts, choose Edit > Preferences >Type (Windows) or Illustrator > Preferences >Type (Mac OS). Enter the values you want in the Size/Leading, Baseline Shift, and Tracking text boxes, and click OK.

Keys for Using Panels.

51

This is not a complete list of keyboard shortcuts. This table lists only those shortcuts that are not displayed in menu commands or tool tips.

Result	Windows Shortcut	Mac OS Shortcut
Set options (except for Actions, Brushes, Swatches, and Symbols panels)	Alt-click New button	Option-click New button
Delete without confirmation (except for Layers panel)	Alt-click Delete button	Option-click Delete button
Apply value and keep text box active	Shift + Enter	Shift + Return
Select range of actions, brushes, layers, links, styles, or swatches	Shift-click	Shift-click
Select noncontiguous actions, brushes, layers (same level only), links, styles, or swatches	Ctrl-click	Command-click
Show/Hide all panels	Tab	Tab
Show/Hide all panels except the Tools panel and Control panel	Shift + Tab	Shift + Tab

Keys for the Actions Panel.

This is not a complete list of keyboard shortcuts. This table lists only those shortcuts that are not displayed in menu commands or tool tips.

Result	Windows Shortcut	Mac OS Shortcut
Expand/Collapse entire hierarchy for action set	Alt-click expansion triangle	Option-click expansion triangle
Set options for action set	Double-click folder icon	Double-click folder icon
Play a single command	Ctrl-click Play Current Selection button	Command-click Play Current Selection button
Begin recording actions without confirmation	Alt-click New Action button	Option-click New Action button

Keys for the Brushes Panel.

This is not a complete list of keyboard shortcuts. This table lists only those shortcuts that are not displayed in menu commands or tool tips.

Result	Windows Shortcut	Mac OS Shortcut

Open Brush Options dialog box	Double-click brush	Double-click brush
Duplicate brush	Drag brush to New Brush button	Drag brush to New Brush button

Keys for the Character and Paragraph Panels.

This is not a complete list of keyboard shortcuts. This table lists only those shortcuts that are not displayed in menu commands or tool tips.

Result	Windows Shortcut	Mac OS Shortcut
Increase/decrease the selected value by a small increment	Up Arrow or Down Arrow	Up Arrow or Down Arrow
Increase/decreases the selected value by a large increment	Shift + Up Arrow or Down Arrow	Shift + Up Arrow or Down Arrow
Highlight the font name field in the Character panel	Ctrl + Alt + Shift + F	Command + Option + Shift + F

Keys for the Color Panel.

This is not a complete list of keyboard shortcuts. This table lists only those shortcuts that are not displayed in menu commands or tool tips.

Result	Windows Shortcut	Mac OS Shortcut
Select the complement for the current color fill/stroke	Ctrl-click color bar	Command-click color bar
Change the nonactive fill/stroke	Alt-click color bar	Option-click color bar
Select the complement for the nonactive fill/stroke	Ctrl + Alt-click color bar	Command + Option-click color bar
Select the inverse for the current fill/stroke	Ctrl + Shift-click color bar	Command + Shift-click color bar
Select the inverse for the nonactive fill/stroke	Ctrl + Shift + Alt-click color bar	Command + Shift + Option-click color bar
Change the color mode	Shift-click color bar	Shift-click color bar
Move color sliders in tandem	Shift-drag color slider	Shift-drag color slider

Switch between percentage and 0-255 values for RGB	Double-click to right of a numerical field	Double-click to right of a numerical field

Keys for the Gradient Panel.

This is not a complete list of keyboard shortcuts. This table lists only those shortcuts that are not displayed in menu commands or tool tips.

Result	Windows Shortcut	Mac OS Shortcut
Duplicate color stops	Alt-drag	Option-drag
Swap color stops	Alt-drag color stop onto another stop	Option-drag color stop onto another color stop
Apply swatch color to active (or selected) color stop	Alt-click swatch in the Swatches panel	Option-click swatch in the Swatches panel
Reset the gradient fill to default black and white linear gradient	Ctrl-click Gradient Fill box in the Gradient panel	Command-click Gradient Fill box in the Gradient panel
Show/Hide gradient arrow	Ctrl + Alt + G	Command + Option + G

Modify angle and end-point together	Alt-drag end point of gradient annotator	Option-drag end point of gradient annotator
Constrain Gradient tool or Gradient annotator while dragging	Shift-drag	Shift-drag
View Gradient annotator in selected gradient filled object	G	G

This is not a complete list of keyboard shortcuts. This table lists only those shortcuts that are not displayed in menu commands or tool tips.

Result	Windows Shortcut	Mac OS Shortcut
Select all objects on the layer	Alt-click layer name	Option-click layer name
Show/hide all layers but the selected one	Alt-click eye icon	Option-click eye icon

Select Outline/Preview view for the selected layer	Ctrl-click eye icon	Command-click eye icon
Selects Outline/Preview view for all other layers	Ctrl + Alt-click eye icon	Command + Option-click eye icon
Lock/unlock all other layers	Alt-click lock icon	Option-click lock icon
Expand all sublayers to display entire hierarchy	Alt-click expansion triangle	Option-click expansion triangle
Set options as you create new layer	Alt-click New Layer button	Option-click New Layer button
Set options as you create new sublayer	Alt-click New Sublayer button	Option-click New Sublayer button
Place new sublayer at bottom of layer list	Ctrl + Alt-click New Sublayer button	Command + Option-click New Sublayer button
Place layer at top of layer list	Ctrl-click New Layer button	Command-click New Layer button
Place layer below selected layer	Ctrl + Alt-click New Layer button	Command + Option-click New Layer button

Copy the selection to a layer, sublayer, or group	Alt-drag selection	Option-drag selection

Keys for the Swatches Panel.

This is not a complete list of keyboard shortcuts. This table lists only those shortcuts that are not displayed in menu commands or tool tips.

Result	Windows Shortcut	Mac OS Shortcut
Create new spot color	Ctrl-click New Swatch button	Command-click New Swatch button
Create new global process color	Ctrl + Shift-click New Swatch button	Command + Shift-click New Swatch button
Replace swatch with another	Alt-drag a swatch over another	Option-drag a swatch over another

Keys for the Transform Panel.

This is not a complete list of keyboard shortcuts. This table lists only those shortcuts that are not displayed in menu commands or tool tips.

Result	Windows Shortcut	Mac OS Shortcut
Apply a value and keep focus in edit field	Shift + Enter	Shift + Return
Apply a value and copy object	Alt + Enter	Option + Return
Apply a value and scale option proportionately for width or height	Ctrl + Enter	Command + Return

Keys for the Transparency Panel.

This is not a complete list of keyboard shortcuts. This table lists only those shortcuts that are not displayed in menu commands or tool tips.

Result	Windows Shortcut	Mac OS Shortcut
Change mask to grayscale image for editing	Alt-click on mask thumbnail	Option-click on mask thumbnail
Disable opacity mask	Shift-click on mask thumbnail	Shift-click on mask thumbnail
Re-enable opacity mask	Shift-click on disabled mask thumbnail	Shift-click on disabled mask thumbnail

Increase/decrease opacity in 1% increments	Click opacity field + Up Arrow or Down Arrow	Click opacity field + Up Arrow or Down Arrow
Increase/decrease opacity in 10% increments	Shift-click opacity field + Up Arrow or Down Arrow	Shift-click opacity field + Up Arrow or Down Arrow

Function Keys.

This is not a complete list of keyboard shortcuts. This table lists only those shortcuts that are not displayed in menu commands or tool tips.

Result	Windows Shortcut	Mac OS Shortcut
Invoke Help	F1	F1
Cut	F2	F2
Copy	F3	F3
Paste	F4	F4
Show/hide Brushes panel	F5	F5
Show/hide Color panel	F6	F6
Show/hide Layers panel	F7	F7

Create new symbol	F8	F8
Show/hide Info panel	Ctrl + F8	Command + F8
Show/hide Gradient panel	Ctrl + F9	Command + F9
Show/hide Stroke panel	Ctrl + F10	Command + F10
Show/hide Attributes panel	Ctrl + F11	Command + F11
Revert	F12	F12
Show/hide Graphic Styles panel	Shift + F5	Shift + F5
Show/hide Appearance panel	Shift + F6	Shift + F6
Show/hide Align panel	Shift + F7	Shift + F7
Show/hide Transform panel	Shift + F8	Shift + F8
Show/hide Pathfinder panel	Shift + Ctrl + F9	Shift + Command + F9
Show/hide Transparency panel	Shift + Ctrl + F10	Shift + Command + F10

Show/hide Symbols panel	Shift + Ctrl + F11	Shift + Command + F11
Show/hide perspective grid	Ctrl+Shift+I	Command+Shift+I

Applies to: *Adobe Illustrator CC.*

Customer's Page.

This page is for customers who enjoyed Adobe Illustrator CC Keyboard Shortcuts.

Our beloved and respectable reader, we thank you very much for your patronage. Please we will appreciate it more if you rate and review this book; that is if it was helpful to you. Thank you.

Download Our EBooks Today For Free.

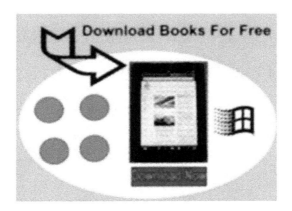

In order to appreciate our customers, we have made some of our titles available at 0.00. They are totally free. Feel free to get a copy of the free titles.

Here are books we give to our customers free of charge:

(A) For Keyboard Shortcuts in Windows check:

Windows 7 Keyboard Shortcuts.

(B) For Keyboard Shortcuts in Office 2016 for Windows check:

Word 2016 Keyboard Shortcuts For Windows.

(C) For Keyboard Shortcuts in Office 2016 for Mac check:

OneNote 2016 Keyboard Shortcuts For Macintosh.

Follow this link to download any of the titles listed above for free.

Note: Feel free to download them from our website or your favorite bookstore today. Thank you.

Other Books By This Publisher.

Titles for single programs under Shortcut Matters Series are not part of this list.

S/N	Title	Series
Series A: Limits Breaking Quotes.		
1	Discover Your Key Christian Quotes	Limits Breaking Quotes
Series B: Shortcut Matters.		
1	Windows 7 Shortcuts	Shortcut Matters
2	Windows 7 Shortcuts & Tips	Shortcut Matters
3	Windows 8.1 Shortcuts	Shortcut Matters
4	Windows 10 Shortcut Keys	Shortcut Matters
5	Microsoft Office 2007 Keyboard Shortcuts For Windows.	Shortcut Matters
6	Microsoft Office 2010 Shortcuts For Windows.	Shortcut Matters
7	Microsoft Office 2013 Shortcuts For Windows.	Shortcut Matters
8	Microsoft Office 2016 Shortcuts For Windows.	Shortcut Matters
9	Microsoft Office 2016 Keyboard Shortcuts For Macintosh.	Shortcut Matters
10	Top 11 Adobe Programs Keyboard Shortcuts	Shortcut Matters
11	Top 10 Email Service Providers Keyboard Shortcuts	Shortcut Matters
12	Hot Corel Programs Keyboard Shortcuts	Shortcut Matters

13	Top 10 Browsers Keyboard Shortcuts	Shortcut Matters
14	Microsoft Browsers Keyboard Shortcuts.	Shortcut Matters
15	Popular Email Service Providers Keyboard Shortcuts	Shortcut Matters
16	Professional Video Editing with Keyboard Shortcuts.	Shortcut Matters
17	Popular Web Browsers Keyboard Shortcuts.	Shortcut Matters

Series C: Teach Yourself.

1	Teach Yourself Computer Fundamentals	Teach Yourself
2	Teach Yourself Computer Fundamentals Workbook	Teach Yourself

Series D: For Painless Publishing

1	Self-Publish it with CreateSpace.	For Painless Publishing
2	Where is my money? Now solved for Kindle and CreateSpace	For Painless Publishing
3	Describe it on Amazon	For Painless Publishing